The Squire and the Scroll

A TALE OF THE REWARDS OF A PURE HEART

Dedication:
To my husband, Randy —
squire, knight and prince.
May your cry continue to turn captive hearts
from stone to flesh.
"For the Lantern and the Scroll!"

Story by Jennie Bishop

Warner Press Kids
educate • nurture • inspire

Paintings by Preston McDaniels

Text ©2004 by Jennie Bishop   Illustrations ©2004 by Warner Press   ISBN: 978-1-59317-079-0

Published by Warner Press, PO Box 2499, Anderson, IN 46018

Art Direction & Design Layout: John Silvey   Editor: Karen Rhodes   Printed in Singapore
615210113432

*I*n the days when men of valor still guarded kings,
a peaceful kingdom lay silent and dark beneath the stars.

The ruler of that kingdom was kind and strong of heart.
It was this good man's charge to guard the Lantern of Purest Light,
the lamp that brought peace and joy to his kingdom.

*B*ut on this sad and terrible night an enemy of all truth and beauty
swept over the castle on leathery wings, and with dreadful magic
stole away the Lantern that gave freedom to all the kingdom.
The king, the queen, and the princess mourned the loss of the precious lamp,
and so did the humble citizens of the peaceful kingdom.

So treasured by the kingdom was the Lantern,
and so beloved was the king that many young men sought bravely
to retrieve the Purest Light. None of them returned.
As one by one the sons of the kingdom disappeared,
the people began to despair.

*A*t last the king was left with only his most trusted knight
to be sent on the quest for the Lantern.

"You must journey to the Red Mountains
where our enemies are known to encamp," said the king.
"I fear traps have been set for you along the way,
as we have already lost so many young men.
If you accomplish this task, you will return
to great honor and reward.
But if you do not, our good people will surely perish."

The knight was fearless and did not complain
about the quest upon which the king was sending him.
he took with him his faithful squire.

The squire was a poor boy who had journeyed far to serve the good king, to become a knight,
and to serve the Lantern. he was honest, a man of his word,
and did all that his master asked him to do. his kind parents were not
people of great position, but they had clean hearts and honored
the Lantern of Purest Light as the people of the kingdom did.
They taught their son how to guard his pure heart by the words from a simple scroll.

When the time came for him to leave the village, the boy's mother and father
presented him with a gift, the scroll from which he had been taught.
And the boy promised to honor his parents and the Lantern by living his life
by the five truths in the scroll. Thus, he received a blessing from his mother and father
and the promise of a reward from God in return for faithfully guarding his heart.

As the knight and the squire started on their journey, they spoke of their families. The knight had little remembrance of his parents, but he vaguely recalled that they had also taught him from a scroll.

"As did mine," said the boy, pulling the parchment from his belt, "and it has always strengthened me and kept my heart pure."

Indeed it had, for the boy knew the words of the scroll so well he often dreamt them, and he honored the Lantern by obedience to the scroll in all that he did. The words of the scroll had seen him through many a temptation. But the knight did not remember the words of the scroll.

The knight and his squire soon came upon a wood through which they must pass on their way to the Red Mountains. Where the path left the meadow and split the underbrush they found a bag of wool.

"Fallen from a traveler's wagon, no doubt," said the knight, passing it to the squire. "Keep it in case we have need."

As the two traveled through the shadowy wood, they began to hear sounds
like a rushing brook or wind in the trees.
Deeper in the forest, the sounds became more like whispers
that seemed to come from the plants, the trees, the ground.
Listening intently, the knight and the boy heard evil chants,
warnings to turn back, whisperings that made their hearts faint.

But the boy knew how to guard his ears, for he knew the first command of the scroll,
"Listen only to words that are pure."

"The wool!" the lad shouted, and quickly pulled off some soft tufts for the knight and himself
to stop up their ears. Now courage could not be stolen from the knight or the boy,
and they passed safely through the enchanted wood.

After some time the knight and the squire came to a great hill
too steep for their horses to climb, but there was
a brightly lit tunnel to the other side. A silver shield lay at
the entrance to this passageway, and the knight handed it
to his squire, thinking it might prove helpful to a boy
of less experience than himself.

The knight walked his horse slowly into the passageway,
wary of evildoing. But he was immediately drawn
to the walls of the tunnel that were encrusted
with millions of precious gems.

The boy also saw the gems; but among them, carved in the stone walls,
were evil images and frightening beings that stared from unnatural faces.
In his horror the boy remembered the second rule on his scroll that said simply,
"Let your eyes look straight ahead, fix your gaze directly before you."
Without a second thought, the boy guarded his face with the shield.

The knight, enamored with the precious stones,
was already talking of plans to take some home to the king.

"But sir," whispered the squire,
"do you not see the evil carved all around the beautiful stones?"

The knight looked at the squire behind his shield, then at the wall.
"What? Ah, those. You are a more innocent lad than I thought.
I have seen all these things before in battle, and worse. Are you afraid?"

"Not afraid, sir, but wary," the squire answered wisely.
"And begging pardon, sir, you ought to be as well, for the scroll says..."

"Silence!" shouted the knight, who usually spoke kindly to the boy. "You are only a squire. I have not become a knight because of any scroll."

With that the knight reached up to pluck a gem from the tunnel wall, and suddenly the tunnel was plunged into darkness!

The squire's horse was startled, and ran.
The young man saw with surprise that through his shield
he could see the tunnel as though it were day.
The squire turned to look back upon the knight
and fought to stop his horse, but to no avail.

*W*hen the horse raced into the light at the other side of the hill the opening in the mountain closed up into a wall of stone. The knight and his horse were lost.

The squire jumped from his horse, breathless, and beat his fists against the rock.
"Open! Open!" he cried, but the doorway did not reappear.
Finally the boy collapsed, grieving the loss of his master.

$\mathcal{T}$hen the squire noticed again the scroll in his belt, and grasped it tightly. "This scroll has led me safely thus far. I believe it will lead me further still."

With great faith he straightened his back and went forward, his mind made up. He had settled in his heart that he would do his best to complete the quest and rescue the Lantern. Even if his own life were required he would complete it for the sake of the kingdom, and for the honor of his master, the knight.

The path was dusty and the journey long. Soon the thirsty squire came to a small lake where a flask stood near the shore. Immediately the third rule of the scroll came to his mind: "Keep the unclean far from your lips to guard the wellspring of your life."

The squire did not know if the pond water was safe to drink, or if the liquid in the flask was refreshment or poison. For some time he walked along the edge of the water, praying patiently for wisdom to come.

Suddenly, the sun which had been concealed by clouds broke through, revealing that the water was full of dead fish and other animals that had lost their lives to its poison. The same glint of light revealed etched words on the flask that spelled PURE. The squire thanked God and drank gratefully. Again the words of the scroll had brought wisdom and saved his life.

It was not surprising to the young man when he came upon a fork in the road, nor was he surprised by the boots that sat on the ground before it. "Rule number four," he whispered. "Make level paths for your feet and take only ways that are firm."

Now one of the paths looked so wet it could well be quicksand that would swallow him up; the other looked dry. But as the squire studied the boots, he thought, "Why would I need boots for a dry path? I believe I ought to take the path that seems a risk. For the wool, the shield, and the flask lead me aright."

Sure enough, when the squire stepped on the wet ground, it was hard as rock. And as he walked further on, he glanced to his side and saw a poor hare wander onto the dry trail and sink into the land that looked solid.

*S*oon the young man stood before the Red Mountains that glowed with an unearthly fire.
Stifling vapors rose up and surrounded a yawning chasm
that led to the dangerous, deep caverns inside.

The squire sniffed the air as his hand went to the parchment at his side. "The scroll says,
'Breathe only that which is pure.'" he looked around, discovered a single beautiful flower
that stood by the entrance to the cave, and plucked it.

holding the bloom close to his face, the squire breathed the scent
of the flower and was able to pass safely through the smoke
to the caves inside the mountain.

In a great hallway that wound down,
down into the earth, the squire found himself
between statues of stone on his right and left.

"The knight!" whispered the squire. his companion was in
the same pose as he had last been seen, reaching for
the precious stones on the walls of the tunnel of light.

"Many must have fallen because of their eyes," thought the squire,
seeing all the lifted hands. Then, with a gasp, he cried,
"And there is the Lantern!"

"There is a price for the Lantern," a voice suddenly hissed.

W hat price?" asked the squire, facing the dragon squarely though his heartbeat thundered in his chest.

"Your scroll," snapped the dragon. "Your scroll is my price.
Give it to me and I shall return the Lantern to your people."

But the wise squire did not believe the creature, for dragons are known to be untrustworthy.
"Give you the scroll which has served me well all my life? Never!" said the boy.

And as he spoke the ground began to tremble and crack,
fire and brimstone steaming up from the deep places of the earth.

"Give me the scroll!" shrieked the dragon, drawing itself to its full height,
"or you will be consumed by the flames!"

"The scroll has always served me well,"
answered the boy, "and it will serve me now!"

And indeed, as he pulled the parchment
from his belt, the scroll was transformed
before the young man's very eyes
into a fearsome double-edged sword.

"For the Lantern and the scroll!" shouted the squire,
and he plunged the sword into the dragon's body.

When the squire pulled his sword from the dragon's lifeless form, it immediately became a scroll again. As the dragon sank into the burning chasm, the figures in the great hallway began to move. Those with lifted arms now seemed to be stretching after a long sleep. The knight came to himself and knelt before the squire, begging his forgiveness.

"I could not guard my eyes," said the knight, ashamed. "But you kept yourself pure. So I promise to you my reward for my life and for the kingdom you have honored."

The squire helped the knight up and embraced him. He remembered the reward that his parents had spoken of.

"We are brothers," said the squire. "Forgiveness is yours."

What a procession all these long-captured sons made
behind the squire as he returned to the castle,
leading them all on the right paths!
And when the travelers came to the tunnel,
it was open, and the Lantern showed the way.
The evil images had now disappeared,
and the gems fell from the walls
as treasure to be gathered for the king and his kingdom.

The celebration that followed the squire's joyous return was unlike any the kingdom had ever seen.
Kneeling before the king, the squire was knighted as he had always dreamed.

"Let us never again forget," the king said to all present,
"how the scroll has served us, and how this good knight returned our Lantern because of it."

"Because of his bravery and his devotion to the Lantern and to the scroll,
he will have my daughter for a wife and rule my kingdom one day.
For who better would guard the Lantern of Purest Light
than one with a heart kept pure?"

A shout went up from the people,
for they were in agreement with their king.

*B*eyond knighting the young squire, the king instituted a new order of protectors: the Knights of the Lantern. The knight who had trained the young squire became its captain. These men dedicated themselves to the words of the scroll and to the defense of the Lantern. It became the goal of many young men of the kingdom to live by the scroll and to one day serve the king in these positions of honor.

As for the knight and the princess, they could not have been happier,
for the princess had devoted herself to the words of the scroll as well,
and so they were a delight to each other.

And when the two were gifted with a son, the knight taught him from the scroll
so that he would one day be ready to defend the kingdom and the Lantern.
For who knows but that another dragon might arise in this young boy's time,
to come and steal the light?

how can a young man keep his way pure?
By living according to your word.   Psalm 119:9 (NIV)